CHILDREN DID YOU KNOW
EASTER BUNNY BELIEVES

written by:
Sharon Kizziah-Holmes
&
Norma Eaton

Illustrated by:
Carlos Lemos

© Copyright © 2018 by Sharon Kizziah-Holmes
Illustrations by Carlos Lemos
All art copyright © 2018
All Rights Reserved

This is a work of fiction. No part of this book may be reproduced or transmitted or transferred in any form or by any means, graphic, electronic or mechanical, including photocopying, recording, taping or by any information storage retrieval system, without the permission in writing by the author.
Any resemblance to actual people and events is purely coincidental.

Kids Book Press
an imprint of A & S Publishing
A & S Holmes, Inc.

ISBN: 978-1945669507

"Hi, kids. Do you know who I am?"

"Yeah!" one said with excitement. "You're the Easter Bunny."

"That's right, I am, and this is my son." He held the little rabbit's hand. "Cute, huh?"

"Do you know this coming Sunday is Easter?"

They all excitedly yelled, "Yes!"

"What is the first thing that comes to your mind when you think of Easter?"

"Candy!" one said.

Another replied, "You, Easter Bunny!"

This is what the bunny feared. Some of the children may not know the true meaning of Easter. "Well, I deliver Easter baskets full of goodies, but there is something more important I need to tell you about Easter."

"But before we begin, I want to let you know, after I get too old to deliver baskets of candy and gifts to children, this little fellow will take my place."

One boy asked, "Will he be big like you? What's his name?" The boy knelt down to pet the younger bunny.

The big rabbit chuckled. "Yes, he'll be big like me then, and his name will become Easter Bunny. The same as when I took my father's name when I became of age. For now, though, you may call him Fuzzy."

One said, "'Cause his fur is fuzzy."

A little girl stood up and cocked her head to one side. "What's your real name, Mr. Bunny?"

The big rabbit rubbed his belly. "You can call me Hairy...for obvious reasons, or because rabbits are also called hares." Hairy liked to make the children giggle.

Mrs. Brown, their teacher, held her hand up to quiet the merriment. "Children, I invited Easter Bunny here to remind you how Easter began many, many years ago, so listen carefully."

Hairy cleared his throat. "Do you all know who God is?"

"He is our Lord and Savior and He lives in heaven," one little girl answered.

"Yes, He does. Did you know He had a son? Just like I have a son, and like God does, I love my boy very much. God's son's name is Jesus. You all know Jesus, don't you?"

"I've a picture of Jesus on my bedroom wall," a girl said.

One boy said, "We know Jesus. Mrs. Brown tells us about him all the time."

Hairy pointed to the picture of Jesus on the Sunday school room wall. "God loves his son just like your mommy and daddy love you. He cherished Jesus but God made a great sacrifice for me, you and all of mankind. Does anyone know what that sacrifice was?"

A girl answered. "When Jesus died on the cross?"

"Yes. That is the day we now call Good Friday. On Sunday Jesus rose from the tomb where He was buried and went to heaven to be with God. Today we call the day He arose Easter Sunday, or some call it Resurrection Day. God's sacrifice wiped away all our sins and gave us a pathway to heaven."

"Was Jesus mad at the bad people who made Him die?"

Hairy smiled. "Jesus forgave them. They just did not believe He was the Son of God even though Jesus showed them through various miracles He performed in His short life. Like turning water into wine, giving a blind man sight, walking on water-- many things."

The boy then smiled. "Jesus is a nice man."

Hairy laughed quietly. "He sure is and we need to be happy for what He did for us and be glad to celebrate Easter."

Mrs. Brown took a seat beside Fuzzy. "Tell us about some of the symbols of Easter we celebrate with each year, please."

Hairy said, "For instance, an egg symbolizes the tomb where Jesus was buried. Baby chicks are the symbol of new life or rebirth. Now days in your baskets I bring yummy candy eggs of all flavors, but they still mean the same thing. We are reborn when we accept God and Jesus as our Lord and Savior."

"The Easter Lily is white and represents the purity of Jesus. It is a flower that grew in the Garden of Gethsemane where Jesus prayed before He was crucified. It is also the symbol of His resurrection."

"What else," one of the children asked.

"Well, the lamb became the symbol of Jesus, his sacrifice of life. After His resurrection, as you will read in the bible verse John 1:29 – The next day John saw Jesus coming toward him and said, "Look, the Lamb of God, who takes away the sin of the world!"

A little boy said, "Jesus is awesome!"

"That He is," the bunny replied.

"Why do I have to get a new dress for Easter. Sometimes it makes me itch."

Hairy led the laughter in the room at the young girl's question. "Easter hats and the new clothes you get to wear on Easter Sunday symbolize new life. This new life was presented through the death and resurrection of Jesus Christ."

"Do any of you like butterflies?" All at one time, the children said yes so Hairy continued. "Then allow me to explain that the beautiful butterfly's life cycle is a very important symbol of Easter. It represents the life of Jesus Christ.

"The caterpillar stage of the butterfly stands for Jesus' life on Earth. When the caterpillar hangs upside down on a twig or leaf, it spins a silky cocoon around itself. This signifies the time Jesus was crucified and His burial.

"Then the beautiful butterfly emerges and you could say, boys and girls, this is the butterfly's way of rising from the dead in a glorified body, just like Jesus did." The kids began to applaud and the bunny was pleased.

"Any questions?"

"Do rabbits go to heaven like people do?" a very young girl asked.

"I sure hope so. I'm planning on it, anyway."

"Good. I want to see you there one day."

"Me, too," said another child.

"Me, three!"

The Easter Bunny smiled wide as the children each counted off a number all the way to eleven. That was all of the children in the class. Then Hairy heard another voice.

"Me, twelve!"

He looked up to see Fuzzy standing in the middle of the floor with his paw raised high in the air. Laughter once again filled the room. Hairy's heart was happy.

Smiling, Mrs. Brown rose and turned to the class. "Let's all thank Easter Bunny for coming and telling us about Easter."

Hairy heard…thank you, Mr. Bunny…thank you, Easter Bunny…Thank you, Hairy and many more from every direction. Even a 'thanks, Dad,' in the background.

"You're welcome everyone. I want you to continue to be excited about your Easter celebrations: dying Easter eggs, Easter egg hunts, Easter parades, dinner with your family and friends, maybe even singing songs! Have a joyous time and especially have fun being surprised at what I bring in your baskets next Sunday morning.

"However, you must always remember Easter is not only about the symbols we talked about today. It's a celebration of Jesus's resurrection and what He did for us."

"You won't see me Easter morning, I'm sneaky that way. But you'll know I've been there when you see what I brought you."

He and Fuzzy waved from the doorway. "You all have as much fun as each day can bring, but above all, think of what's said in the bible in John 3:16, "For God so loved the world, that He gave His only begotten Son, that whosoever believeth in Him should not perish, but have everlasting life."

About the Author

Sharon Kizziah-Holmes

I live in the beautiful Ozarks with my husband and two Cocker Spaniels, Dude and Lacy. I have seventeen grandkids and two great grands...that's right, I'm too young, I know... =) However, I love each and every one of them with all my heart and wouldn't change a thing.

My interest in writing novels came in the early 1990's. A friend suggested we write a book together, so I took her up on it. I joined writing groups and a whole new world opened up for me. I'm still a member of many writing groups. I absolutely love writing, editing, publishing and teaching the basics of writing to others.

My first children's book was written with other authors. Thanks to Michael and Betty Edging for including me in the Camouflage Santa Claus endeavor. That is what inspired me to write 'Children Did You Know, Santa Believes'.

Be sure to get your 'Children Did You Know, Santa Believes' coloring book!

Coming in the spring of 2016, 'Children Did You Know, the Easter Bunny Believes', also with companion coloring book.

Happy Reading and Happy Easter!

Sharon Kizziah-Holmes

About the Author

Norma Eaton

Norma is the author of romance novels, short stories and magazine articles. She was a long-time member of Ozarks Romance Authors as well as other writing groups. She and her husband reside in Springfield, Missouri and sing gospel music at various venues in and around the Branson/Springfield area. She values her love of God and family above all else.

About the Illustrator

Carlos Lemos

Carlos is a freelance illustrator, cartoonist and caricaturist. He started his career in 2006, then in 2010 he became a Visual Art teacher, doing workshops for high schools and colleges.

In 2014 he started an Atelier about comics and caricatures. He makes presentations in Uruguay and Argentina. The workshops also include learning about the creative process.

Over the years, Carlos has illustrated over thirty children's books for people from around the world. Some of his comics include:

"Verano". An anthology with a summer theme.

"Grimorilo do Plata", a dark themed graphic novel.

"Crononautas", a young adult sci-fi graphic novel.

"Carpincho", a historical web comic to the project Ceibal (one computer per child of the public education in his country)and freelance comics for individuals.

He lives in the capital city of Uruguay, Montevideo, with the love of his life and their daughter. He enjoys spending time on the beach with his family, and though he loves his work, Carlos is most proud of being a father.

www.ingramcontent.com/pod-product-compliance
Lightning Source LLC
Chambersburg PA
CBHW040027050426
42453CB00002B/30